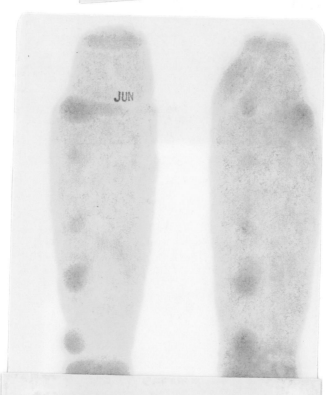

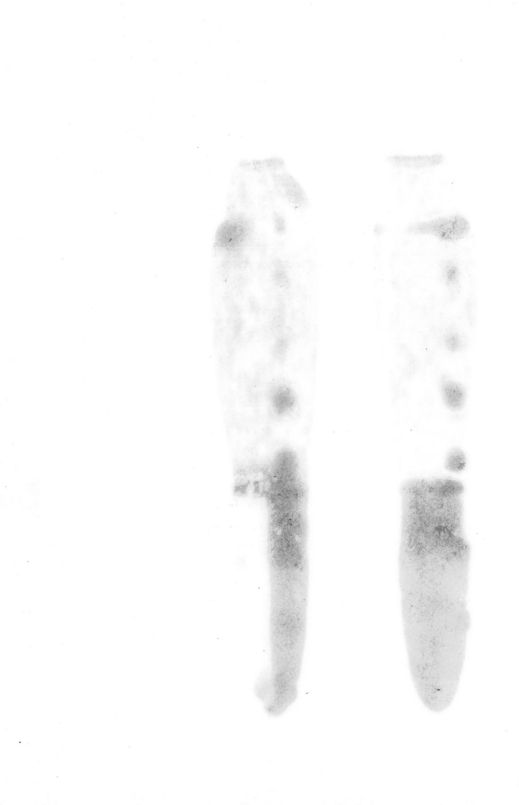

Louis Pasteur and Microbiology

Pasteurization, which has almost wiped out tuberculosis spread through milk, is named after Louis Pasteur. This giant of scientific discovery has saved untold lives through his study of the cause and prevention of infectious diseases, especially anthrax, diphtheria, cholera and rabies. His work on silkworm disease saved the silk industry of France. His work on fowl cholera saved French farmers a fortune and his research on the fermentation of wine and beer is said to have saved more money than the reparations claimed by Germany after the Franco-Prussian war.

Louis Pasteur was the son of a tanner. He was born in Dôle, France, in 1822. After his schooldays, he went to Paris to study under the famous chemist Jean Baptiste Dumas, and his first discovery, made when only twenty-six, was that some chemical crystals rotated light in one direction and others in another. This started the science of stereochemistry and made him famous at once. He later became Professor of Physics at Dijon, and after some time at Strasbourg and Lille he went back to Paris, where he did much of his work on silkworm disease, anthrax and rabies. Although crippled by a stroke when only forty-six, he went on working, this time on the prevention of infection in hospitals. Later came his work on anthrax, fowl cholera, rabies and diphtheria. Microbiology was now a well-established science.

Professor Winner tells the story of this remarkable man with enthusiasm, and in simple non-technical language recaptures the excitement of his great moments of discovery. The book contains more than forty illustrations, a glossary, reading list, date chart and index.

Pioneers of Science and Discovery

Louis Pasteur
and Microbiology

H I Winner M.A., M.D., F.R.C.P.,
F.R.C.PATH.

Professor of Medical Microbiology,
Charing Cross Hospital Medical School,
University of London.

Other Books in this Series

To Nina, Jonathan, and Simon

ISBN 85078 122 1
Copyright © 1974 by H I Winner
Second impression 1978
Third impression 1980
First published in· 1974 by
Wayland Publishers Ltd.,
49 Lansdowne Place, Hove, East Sussex BN3 1HF
Printed and bound in Great Britain at The Pitman Press, Bath

Contents

HAROLD I. WINNER was educated at St. Pauls' School, and Downing College, Cambridge, and qualified at University College Hospital Medical School in London. He is now Professor of Medical Microbiology in the University of London at Charing Cross Hospital Medical School, and Consultant Bacteriologist at Charing Cross Hospital. He is a Founder Fellow of the Royal College of Pathologists.

List of Illustrations

Foreword

This book has been written to introduce young people to the life and work of one of the great pioneers of medicine. It has been a pleasure to write, for Pasteur was such a wonderful man. I hope that some of this pleasure has come across in the book.

My task was made easier by the cheerful hard work of my secretary, Miss Morag Campbell. My colleague Dr. Hilary Andrews very kindly read the manuscript and made many helpful suggestions. I am most grateful to these two ladies.

March 1973   H. I. Winner

Introduction

"I think continually of those who were truly great . . .
Near the snow, near the sun, in the highest fields
See how these names are fêted by the waving grass
And by the streamers of white cloud
And whispers of wind in the listening sky.
The names of those who in their lives fought for life,
Who wore at their hearts the fire's centre.
Born of the sun, they travelled a short while towards
    the sun
And left the vivid air signed with their honour."

Stephen Spender

"Lives of great men all remind us
We can make our lives sublime,
And, departing, leave behind us
Footprints on the sands of time;—

Footprints, that perhaps another,
Sailing o'er life's solemn main,
A forlorn and shipwrecked brother,
Seeing, shall take heart again."

Longfellow

There are few men and women in history who are universally acknowledged to have been truly and completely great. There must have been flaws in their character somewhere, but they are hidden by the immense good of the example of their life and work. They were noted not only for their tremendous achievements but for their beauty of character. Leonardo Da Vinci was such a person. Louis Pasteur was another.

In these cynical days we are apt to regard with suspicion any claim to perfection. But this can be taken too far. It is rightly a source of inspiration to ordinary people like ourselves that such great men and women have existed, and their examples can help us in our daily lives.

In the case of Leonardo, all who knew him testified to his delightful and generous character. Similarly with Louis Pasteur. The remarkable thing is that Pasteur is still so close to us. He died less than a century ago. He lived in a terrible age in France— an age of revolution and civil war, of grinding poverty, of needless slaughter.

It was an age of corruption at every social level, of cowardice, deceit and faithlessness. It was the age when two of the greatest French novelists, Balzac and Zola, took the lid off the wickedness of life in their country, stinking as it was with lust and avarice.

It was certainly not an age which was likely to encourage or even recognize human perfection without a sneering suggestion that an appearance of goodness was merely a façade. Nevertheless it is most remarkable that no one has ever suggested that Pasteur was anything but a person of the utmost honour, integrity and kindliness, as well as having been intellectually one of the greatest men who ever lived.

I. *Early Life and Education*

Jean Joseph Pasteur, the father of Louis, was born in Besançon in 1791. He became a tanner, like his father and grandfather before him. He was conscripted into the army in the Peninsular War of 1811. After the war, he returned peaceably to his work at Besançon. He was then a reserved man, careful and slow in his dealings with people. He fell in love with a young girl, whose character, in contrast, was active, enthusiastic, and full of imagination. The couple were married in 1815, and migrated to Dôle.

Louis Pasteur in 1884

Their first child lived for only a few months. In 1818 they had a daughter and four years later, on Friday, December 27th 1822, Louis Pasteur was born. Two more daughters followed.

For family reasons Jean Joseph Pasteur had to leave Dôle to live at Marnoz, where he again set up as a tanner. However, the family did not stay there very long. There was a tannery to let in the nearby town of Arbois, with a little house and a yard with pits for the preparation of the skins. Here the Pasteurs settled.

Young Louis went first to the Primary School and then to the College. He was then a small boy, and became a good average pupil. He won several prizes, but was not especially outstanding. During his holidays he would go on fishing parties with his friends. He was also very good at drawing, and produced some pastels which were so good that his friends nicknamed him "the artist."

Perhaps the first person to realize the divine spark in Louis was the headmaster of his school, Monsieur Romanet. He often used to take the young Louis for strolls around the college playground, talking to him about what he might do in the future.

When he was sixteen, the time came to discuss Louis' further education. A friend of his father, Captain Barbier, kindly offered to look after Louis if he went to school in Paris. Joseph Pasteur hesitated, but eventually agreed that Louis should go. His close school friend, Jules Vercel, was also going. However, the expedition was not a success. Louis grew very homesick, and after only a few weeks his father came to Paris to take him home.

Back in Arbois, Louis again took up drawing in pastels, and produced a little portrait gallery of the friends of the family.

Pasteur's mother and father painted by Louis at the age of sixteen

Pasteur's sundial, which he built in 1879, overlooking the courtyard of his college at Arbois (*left*)

The College at Besançon (*right*)

The problem of his higher education remained. Pasteur decided to go to the College at Besançon, 40 kilometres from his home. While he was there, he was able to see his family often and he did very well. He took the degree of Bachelor of Letters in August 1840. At the end of the summer holidays the headmaster of the Royal College of Besançon offered him the post of preparation master. He started this job in January 1841.

Louis Pasteur was now a serious and mature young man. It soon became clear that in time he would have to go back to Paris for his further education. Obviously, there were greater opportunities in the capital, and life was cheaper for a student there. In August 1842 Pasteur passed the examinations which allowed him to apply for admission to the Ecole Normale.

In October he set off with a friend. Once in Paris, he entered the Barbet boarding school, where he was a part-time teacher as well as a student. He attended classes of the Lycée St. Louis, and also went regularly to the Sorbonne to hear the lectures of Professor

Dumas, the renowned chemist. Dumas was one of the few teachers able to inspire enthusiasm as well as impart knowledge, and had an enormous influence on Pasteur.

Pasteur settled down well to this new life, working hard and happily. He made himself so useful that he was soon able to pay his own way. At the end of the school year 1843, the results of his examinations were brilliant—several distinctions and a first prize in physics.

Pasteur was fourth on the list of those admitted to the Ecole Normale, where he started work with enthusiasm. On his half holidays he arranged to give lessons on physical science at M. Barbet's school.

Professor Jean Baptiste Dumas

Louis had grown into a grave, quiet, rather shy young man, tall and thoughtful, but full of dash and fire under this reserved façade. He read widely and his letters to his family show that he was very happy at this time.

La Sorbonne, the famous university in Paris where Pasteur went to hear Dumas' lectures

2. *Crystals and Light Rays*

Pasteur was in the habit of taking long walks in the Luxembourg Gardens with his companion Chappuis. On these walks they discussed everything—philosophy, history, and science. One day Pasteur began to talk about tartaric acid, which had been discovered in 1770 by the Swedish chemist Scheele. When polarized light is passed through solutions of tartaric acid, the solution can turn the plane of the light to the right. So can solutions of ordinary sugar and crystals of certain quartzes. Some other substances, such as turpentine or quinine, rotate polarized light to the left. A rather mysterious substance called racemic acid had been studied by Gay-Lussac and Berzelius. Chemically it looked similar to tartaric acid, but it did not rotate the plane of polarized light at all. Pasteur wanted to find out more about this substance. No one knew why it differed from tartaric acid in

The square in front of the Sorbonne

The Luxembourg Palace Gardens,
Paris

failing to polarize the light passed through it. This is typical of the kind of problem which Pasteur studied during the next few years.

Another problem in which Pasteur was interested was dimorphism. Some substances produce different kinds of crystals if different methods of preparation are used. For example, sulphur melted in a crucible produces crystals which are quite unlike those obtained from solutions of sulphur in carbon disulphide. Such substances are called dimorphic, and Pasteur studied the reasons why the different forms occur.

During the revolutionary year of 1848, Pasteur found himself in Paris. He joined the National Guard, and in an outburst of enthusiasm gave all his savings to the cause of the Republic.

Meanwhile he continued his work as a teacher and his research in chemistry. His absorption in the problem of tartaric acid soon bore fruit. He discovered that racemic acid was made up of two kinds of crystals which differed in only one respect. Some rotated the plane of polarized light to the right and others to the left. They were of a similar asymmetrical shape, and in fact were mirror images of one another. Pasteur had the idea that racemic acid did not rotate the plane of light at all because it was a mixture of equal quantities of these two types of acid. The two kinds of rotation cancelled one another out.

The importance of this discovery was that it showed that similar organic chemicals could exist in two forms which differed only in that their crystals were mirror images and rotated light in different directions. We know now that the polarization happens not only in crystals but also in solutions of the substances. The actual molecules of the two forms are mirror images of one another in three dimensions.

As a result of his brilliant work Pasteur was made Professor of Physics at the Lycée in Dijon. He arrived there in November 1848. However, he did not stay long, for in January he was appointed Professor of Chemistry at Strasbourg.

The new Rector of the Academy of Strasbourg was named Laurent. He was an amiable and warm-hearted man. He and his wife and their two un-married daughters welcomed Pasteur as a frequent guest to their home.

Only two weeks after Pasteur arrived in Strasbourg, he made up his mind to marry the second daughter. His proposal was accepted, and the young couple were married on May 29th 1849.

Strasbourg

A page from Pasteur's laboratory notebook showing some of his work on tartaric acid and its chemical compounds (right)

Cristallisation d'un mélange de bitartrate et de
bimalate d'ammon.

~~10 gr. bitartrate~~ Je fais dissoudre   8.350   bitartrate droit
~~20 gr. bimalate~~   Total = 15.900   ~~7.550~~   bimalate actif
~~100 f. eau~~   Les deux poids sont dans les rapports des éq^ts
des deux sels acides. 70 gr. d'eau suffisent bien pour dissoudre
le mélange à chaud. On évapore alors la solution à l'éb^on [il est à noter que
150 p. d'eau à chaud ont en de la peine à dissoudre 10 gr. bit^t + 20 gr. bim.
ou 75 gr. d'eau pour 5 gr. bit. + 10 gr. bim. voir p. 22. N'y a
t'il pas il en erreur dans ce cas ci de la p. 22 ce serait à reprendre.] Elle
dépose tout de suite et de pleins angles de cristaux. Je fais redissoudre
exactement à 70 gr. d'eau et je mets à cristalliser. Il y a à la raison du
liquide d. s. cristaux, ce qui prouve qu'on est près de la sursaturation
70 et donc à peu près l'excès d'eau nec. ... il faut pour dissoudre 15,9 d'un
mélange à éq^ts égaux de bimalate et de b. tartrate d'amm.

⟶ La 1re cristallisation (Reprendre fiche 65) déposée le lendemain est très uniforme.
Elle en lames biselées assez larges avec stries parallèles qui annoncent
un clivage facile. Ces cristaux sont identiques pour l'aspect et la
forme (seulement ici plus larges) avec ceux de la 1re crist^on déposée
dans un pareil mélange à éq^ts égaux des 2 sels p. 19. Il me paraît
dès lors certain que c'est le même corps et on a vu p. 19 qu'il
renfermait du bimalate combiné certainement ⟶

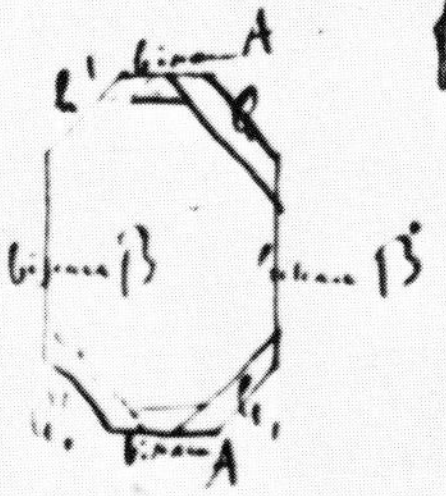

Voici la forme de ces lames : Les faces b', b₂, b', sont 4
fois titraédriques. Mais, clarités d'incidence des deux
faces avec les faces du bimaux A me sont pas étant normales
aux arêtes des bimaux comme cela arrive dans le
bitartrate pur. Je crois que cela est aussi pour
le bimaux B, mais celui-ci est moins net.
Il faut noter que dans le bit. pur le clivage est
vertical et perpend^re à l'arête du bimaux proprement
dit. Dans la figure ci-contre c'est donc le
bimaux B qui ~~sont~~ du véritable bimaux de bit. pur,
en se lassant quitter par le clivage.

fig. 1

3. *The Young Married Professor*

Pasteur's marriage was ideal, largely because Madame Pasteur accepted from the first that the laboratory should come before anything else. She shared Louis' enthusiasms, hopes, anxieties and happinesses, and provided him with the stable and happy home life which was the essential background for his work.

Pasteur's future life was to be intensely active and busy. For such a life a tranquil and stable private background is one of the greatest blessings, whose importance to its fortunate possessors cannot be overestimated. Who can say what would have happened to Louis if he had had a nagging or unfaithful wife?

Admittedly, some famous men do not have happy home lives—Haydn, Abraham Lincoln. Others, like Michelangelo, Leonardo da Vinci and Beethoven, remain unmarried. The achievements of great men and their effectiveness in life result from their temperament, moods and self-confidence, as well as from their abilities. These personal qualities must obviously be affected by the intimate personal circumstances of their lives, of which the most far-reaching and all-pervading is their home background.

Pasteur's study of different varieties of tartaric acid and similar compounds took him on many trips into the old German Empire—Saxony, Trieste, Vienna, Leipzig, Freiberg and Prague. In June 1853, in a telegram to his father, Louis announced that he had transformed tartaric acid into racemic acid artificially in the laboratory. There were now four different tartaric acids: 1. dextro-tartaric acid, which rotates light to the right; 2. laevo-tartaric acid,

Pasteur and his wife in 1884

which rotates light to the left; 3. the mixture of the two, which was optically inactive; and 4. meso-tartaric acid, which was also optically inactive, but could not be separated into two components. This differentiation into four types was a great advance, and for making it Pasteur was awarded the red ribbon of the Legion of Honour.

In Strasbourg, Pasteur moved with his young and growing family into a larger house with a garden. Meanwhile, he went on studying the properties of crystals.

One of his observations was as follows. He broke an octahedral crystal and replaced one of the broken fragments in its mother liquor. It started to get bigger and after a few hours the broken end had resumed its original shape. Pasteur saw a similarity between this strange phenomenon and the healing of wounds in which damaged living tissues resume their original form after a time. The great physiologist Claude Bernard was much struck by this observation of likenesses between two such different happenings. Such recognition of affinity hidden under facts apparently far apart is one of the hallmarks of genius.

Other unexpected similarities between apparently unrelated phenomena stimulated Pasteur to think deeply about objects which were asymmetrical. He came to see dissymmetry, as he called it, everywhere. "The universe is a dissymmetrical whole," was one of his sayings at the time. Another was "Life is dominated by dissymmetrical actions." Meanwhile his work went on with the usual ups and downs experienced by any research scientist.

In September 1854, Pasteur was made Professor and Dean of the new Faculté des Sciences at Lille. This was a big chance for the young scientist, especially as there were many local distilleries where yeast fermentations could be studied.

Pasteur took a broad view of his duties as teacher

and Dean. It was an exciting time for the scientist. The electric telegraph had been invented; this and the other discoveries of modern science resulted in a great growth of industrial technology, which could well be studied in the neighbourhood of Lille. Pasteur took his pupils round factories and foundries and steel and metal works in the industrial areas of France and of the neighbouring Belgium. He felt it was of great importance to show them the relation between the different aspects of applied science.

His approach was optimistic yet practical. He felt that people should work hard to benefit humanity, and should think broadly. "In the field of observation, chance favours only the prepared mind" is a quotation from a speech he made at this time.

In 1857 Pasteur was a candidate for election to the Academy of Sciences. However, he failed to secure the necessary 30 votes. On his return to Lille he set to work on the study of the fermentation of sour milk and showed that it was due to a yeast like the one which fermented beer.

The Ecole Normale in Paris was going through a difficult time, and Pasteur felt that he should go back there. He was appointed to take charge of the administration and direction of scientific studies. The scientific facilities were very poor. However, he cheerfully set out to study alcoholic fermentation. He found that glycerine and succinic acid were unexpected by-products of this process—where did they come from? He turned these problems over in his mind, too cautious to propound theories until the established facts justified them.

This period was marred by the death, in September 1859, of his eldest daughter, from typhoid fever.

4. Microbes and Spontaneous Generation

On January 30th, 1860, the Academy of Science awarded Pasteur the prize for experimental physiology. It was his friend, the great physiologist Claude Bernard, who drew up the report on which this award was based.

Pasteur now started work on the problem of spontaneous generation of microbes. Since the days of Aristotle and Lucretius, many people had believed that microscopic animals could arise spontaneously out of non-living dirt and dust, and the philosophical revival in the middle of the 18th century again raised this problem in scientific circles.

Pasteur's aged teacher Biot had long felt that spontaneous generation did not occur, but had not managed to prove it. He tried to discourage Pasteur from going ahead, thinking that Pasteur would not get anywhere, but would waste a lot of time and energy.

In 1858 Pouchet, Director of the Natural History Museum at Rouen, sent to the Academy of Sciences a paper strongly in favour of spontaneous generation. He proclaimed: "Animals and plants could be generated in a medium absolutely free from atmospheric air, and in which, therefore no germ of organic bodies could have been brought by air." Pasteur thought that Pouchet's work was not conclusive and wrote to him "in experimental science it is always a mistake not to doubt when facts do not compel affirmation—in my opinion the question is not decisively proved. What is there in the air which gives rise to these creatures? Are they germs? Is it a solid? Is it a gas? Is it a fluid? Is it a principle such as ozone? All this is unknown and we have to experiment to find the answers."

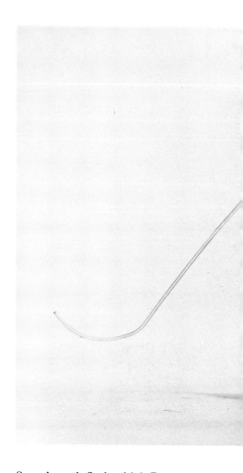

Swan's neck flask which Pasteur used in his studies of spontaneous generation

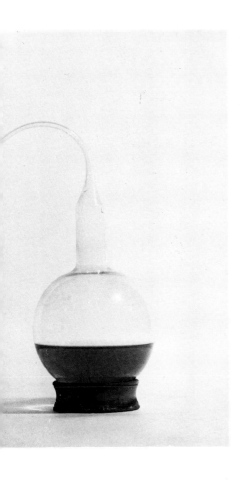

Pasteur plunged with enthusiasm into experimental work. He took a number of 250 cubic centimetre flasks and filled them with a suspension of yeast in water. He then boiled each flask and, while the fluid was still boiling, he closed the pointed opening through which the steam was escaping.

Pasteur divided these flasks into two groups. He broke the necks of one group, so that the surrounding air rushed in bringing with it dust and yeast spores from the atmosphere. He then closed the necks again. The other group he left intact. Yeasts and other moulds grew in the flasks whose necks had been opened and which had thus been contaminated by the surrounding air. Nothing grew in the flasks which had been left sealed. This experiment showed that the development of microbes was not spontaneous, but had obviously been due to contamination. Pasteur backed it up with similar observations, all of which helped to demolish the theory of spontaneous generation. However, it was difficult to convince people that spontaneous generation never occurred—nothing is harder than to prove a negative.

In 1862, Pasteur was elected to the Academy of Sciences. His speeches and lectures at this time contain many wise and memorable passages. Here is an example: "A man of science should think of what will be said of him in the following century, not of the insults or compliments of one day." In January 1864, he declared: "Might not the diseases of wines be caused by organized ferments, by microscopic vegetations, the germs of which would develop when the temperature, atmospheric pressure, and exposure to air would favour their growth in wines?" He was, of course, quite right. Later that year he accepted the offer of the town of Arbois to study wine diseases.

These were a serious economic problem. Pasteur found that by keeping the wine for a short time at a temperature of 50° to 60°C the diseases could be

25

Some of Pasteur's apparatus on show in London in 1947 (*left*)

The physiologist Claude Bernard (*below*)

prevented, and the treatment did not harm the wine. This became standard practice in wine-growing districts—it was the first example of what we now call "Pasteurisation."

5. Silkworms, Wine, Cholera. Pasteur's Illness

In 1865 the silk industry was almost ruined by a serious epidemic among the silkworms. The leaders of the industry asked Jean Baptiste Dumas, now a senator, to draw up a report on their plight. Dumas urged Pasteur to study the problem and try to solve it.

Pasteur hesitated. This was a completely new field for him, he pointed out, and he did not want to leave his department and laboratory in the university. Nonetheless he let himself be persuaded and in 1865 he departed for Alais.

The silkworm disease was a fatal infection. It started on the surface giving rise to little spots looking like pepper grains; hence it was called *pébrine* from *pébré*, the provincial name for pepper. In 1849 there was a disastrous epidemic. A few years later, Italy, Spain and Austria were attacked, and gradually the disease spread further. China was attacked and by 1864 it was only in Japan that healthy seed could be found.

Pasteur started work in Alais trying to grow some microbes from the affected silk worms. No sooner had he begun than he received a telegram telling him that his father was desperately ill. He rushed to Arbois but arrived too late. His father was dead.

Pasteur returned in grief to his studies at Alais. He looked at hundreds of silk chrysalides and moths under the microscope and saw that many of them were diseased. The idea came to him that the disease started in the more mature forms of the worms, which produced diseased eggs which in turn gave rise to diseased chrysalides and moths.

He obtained some healthy moths from Turkey,

Silkworms feeding on young mulberry plants (*above*)

and decided to compare the moths hatched from their eggs with those hatched from diseased eggs.

In the meantime, he went back to his work in Paris, where a further blow struck him. His youngest child, Camille, only two years old, was seriously ill. She died in September 1865, after Pasteur had returned to Arbois.

This was perhaps the most productive period in Pasteur's life. He was busy on many important problems; he was playing a leading role in academic and scientific life and he wrote many important papers and articles.

All this time Pasteur was obsessed by the possibility of finding a connecting link between the "fermentations" or infections which attacked yeasts, those which attacked animals such as moths, and those which attacked human beings.

As usual, his general speculations were interrupted

Napoléon III, Emperor of the French (*right*)

29

by a crisis. In 1865, cholera had travelled from Egypt to Marseilles and then to Paris, and in October that year more than 200 people were dying from it every day. Claude Bernard, Pasteur and Sainte Claire determined to find out if the disease was caused by a microbe. They went into the attics of a hospital just above the cholera ward, and sampled the air. However, they did not grow any microbes which seemed likely to have caused the disease. They then took blood from cholera patients and cultured it, but did not grow any microbes from these specimens either.

This work also was interrupted by a flattering invitation from the Emperor Napoléon III, to come and spend a weekend at the Palace of Compiègne. The Emperor loved science, and Pasteur felt he had to accept. The Emperor gave Pasteur particular attention, and spent much time in private talks with him.

During one of these conversations, Napoléon and the Empress Eugénie told Pasteur they were surprised that he did not try to make money from his work. Pasteur replied: "In France, scientists would consider they lowered themselves by doing so." He was convinced that a man of science would complicate his life, interrupt the flow of his thoughts, and risk paralysing his inventive faculties were he to be able to make money from his discoveries. The conflict would be too deep.

In 1866 the Ministry of Agriculture asked Pasteur to continue his studies on silkworm disease. Pasteur agreed and went away again to the silk producing districts with two colleagues. The three men began by looking for a suitable house where they could set up a laboratory. They found one; it was large enough to hold Pasteur, his family and his pupils. On her way to Alais, Pasteur's daughter Cécile, then twelve years old, fell ill with typhoid fever. She died on May 23rd after a sudden relapse.

After this further calamity, Pasteur returned in sorrow to his research. He put forward the suggestion, which was new at the time, that the silkworm disease was infectious, and said that no eggs should be used that came from infected moths.

In the meantime, Pasteur was editing his book on wines. In order to keep wines free from all germs of disease and make them suitable for storage and for export, he had already shown that it was enough to heat them by the simple process which had become known as Pasteurization. Pasteur did not pay much attention to the talk of old gourmets who said that heating harmed the wines and prevented them from mellowing with age. The ageing of wines, said Pasteur, is due not to fermentation but to slow oxidation, which is in fact encouraged by the heating.

Meanwhile, the work on silkworm disease went ahead. Pasteur showed that infection might occur in one of two ways—either by direct contact between the worms on the same frame, or by soiling of their food by the infected excreta of the worms.

Next year, Pasteur learned that the Grand Prize Medal of the 1867 Exhibition was to be conferred on him for his work on wine. The ceremony took place on July 1st, when Paris looked its best. The central avenue of the Tuileries Gardens, the Place de la Concorde, and the Avenue des Champs Elysées were lined by regiments of infantry, dragoons and guards. The imperial carriage drawn by eight horses, escorted by the Guards in their pale blue uniforms and by the Lancers of the Household, arrived in triumphant array. Many royalties from different countries and notables accompanied the

Drawing from a book by Pasteur on
diseases in silkworms

ÉTUDES

SUR LE VIN

SES MALADIES

CAUSES QUI LES PROVOQUENT

PROCÉDÉS NOUVEAUX

POUR LE CONSERVER ET POUR LE VIEILLIR

PAR M. L. PASTEUR

MEMBRE DE L'INSTITUT

———

ÉTUDES COURONNÉES PAR LE COMITÉ CENTRAL AGRICOLE DE SOLOGNE

PARIS

IMPRIMÉ PAR AUTORISATION DE SON EXC. LE GARDE DES SCEAUX

A L'IMPRIMERIE IMPÉRIALE

———

M DCCC LXVI

Emperor. Another of the eminent men honoured that day was Ferdinand de Lesseps, builder of the Suez Canal.

All this time Pasteur was suffering from a lack of money for his research. He wrote to Napoléon asking for a larger laboratory and more money. The very next day the Emperor wrote to Duruy, the Minister of Public Instruction, strongly supporting Pasteur's request. Duruy agreed and began to draw up plans. Meanwhile Pasteur was invited to Orleans to give a public lecture on his studies on vinegar. This took place on Monday, November 11th, 1866. Pasteur was then the youngest member of the Academy of Science. An account in the local paper describes the scene. "He was of medium height, his face pale, his eyes very bright through his glasses, scrupulously neat in his dress, with a tiny rosette of the Legion of Honour in his buttonhole."

In his famous lecture Pasteur showed that the transformation of wine into vinegar was due to a microscopic fungus, *Mycoderma aceti*. He demonstrated that the mycoderma would multiply profusely in any alcoholic and slightly acid liquid, and would cover a large area of liquid in 48 hours. Floating on the surface, the mycoderma absorbed oxygen from the air, transforming the alcohol into acetic acid.

The year 1867 shows Pasteur, then 45 years old, at the height of his powers. He would start work early in the morning, working on a single problem for several hours. He was thoughtful, almost dreamy, until some action was called for when he at once revealed himself as a man of action. His intuition and imagination were as keen as those of any poet.

At the end of the year Pasteur heard to his consternation that money had been refused for the building of his new laboratory, at a time when millions of francs were being spent on the Opera House. He prepared an article for the *Moniteur*, the official paper, protesting at the cuts made and

Title page of the work on wines and how to keep them free of germs and disease, for which Pasteur was to receive the Grand Prize Medal of the 1867 Exhibition

L. Pasteur

Londres, à 21 avril 1884.

contrasting the poverty of science in France with the large sums devoted to this cause in Germany, Russia, England, Austria, Bavaria and Italy.

The article attacked the Government and the editor of the *Moniteur* became alarmed. He knew that Pasteur would never agree to make any alterations but advised him to show the proofs to Monsieur Conti, Secretary to Napoléon III. Conti considered that the article could not appear in the *Moniteur* and suggested that Pasteur publish it as a booklet. Duruy, the Minister of Public Instruction, approved of Pasteur's general argument, as did the Emperor himself. His campaign had a good effect in that from that time onwards the Emperor consulted him and other leading scientists about the best way to support science in France.

In 1868 the University of Bonn offered Pasteur the degree of M.D. for his work on microbes. Pasteur was delighted and flattered. He greatly admired German higher education, with the liberal support it received, and the intellectual independence of the university teachers. He did not suspect the military side of the German nature. This was the time when Germany was actively preparing for the war with France, much to the concern of some high-ranking French officers, who warned their Government but were ignored—a story with which we have become only too familiar during the present century.

In July 1868 Pasteur heard that the building of his laboratory was about to begin at last. His life was now very full. The results of his researches on silk-worm disease were being actively applied by the silk industry, and those on the spoilage of wine and beer by the brewers. These results were confirmed by a decisive experiment organised by Monsieur de Lapparent, the Director of Naval Construction in the Ministry of Marine. A frigate started on a cruise round the world with a large cargo of wine. This had been heated by Pasteur to kill the mycoderma

Louis Pasteur at the age of sixty-two

and so prevent spoilage. After the long journey the wine was perfect. This demonstrated clearly that it was now possible to ship French wines all over the world without fear of deterioration.

On Monday October 19th, 1868, Pasteur was due to read a treatise to the Academy of Science. In the morning he felt unwell, with a strange tingling on the left side of his body. After lunch he had an alarming shivering fit, but insisted on going to the meeting of the Academy. Madame Pasteur was uneasy about his condition, and went with him as far as the entrance of the institute.

Pasteur read the paper in his usual steady voice and walked back to his home. After a light dinner he went to bed early. Hardly had he got into bed when he felt himself attacked by the same symptoms as earlier in the day. He tried, at first in vain, to speak, but after a few moments he was able to call for help. At once Madame Pasteur sent for their friend Dr. Godélier. Pasteur explained his symptoms, which were those of a gradually increasing cerebral haemorrhage. This rapidly brought complete paralysis of the left side of his body.

For the next few days Pasteur struggled for his life. At times it was thought that there was no hope for him. However, he gradually improved, though the paralysis remained.

All through his illness Pasteur's mind remained clear and lucid, in contrast to his crippled body. His chief regret was that he would die before having completely solved the question of silkworm diseases. During the height of his illness he dictated notes on this and other problems to the friends who hardly left his bedside.

Pasteur was not expected to recover, and the building work on his new laboratory slowed down and almost stopped. When he heard about this Pasteur complained to Napoléon, who personally instructed Monsieur Duruy to make sure that the building should not suffer.

By November 30th Pasteur had improved enough to get out of bed and spend an hour in his armchair. He coolly and calmly took stock of his situation.

He was almost 46 years old and had been working more effectively than ever, but he was now partly paralyzed. He told his wife and daughter he was anxious not to be a burden to them. His chief wish was to carry on with his work.

Most striking was the contrast between his ardent, aspiring and active brain, and his stricken paralyzed body. He read a lot—the works of Pascal, Nicole and Bossuet. *Self-help*, by Samuel Smiles, interested and helped him greatly. His family and friends read to him in the daytime. Many friends visited him. The bulletins continued to tell of his recovery.

Pasteur was not the man to stay at home as a convalescent a moment longer than necessary. Exactly three months after his stroke, he set out for Alais to see how the work on silkworm disease was going on. A laboratory was improvised, and from his sofa or his bed Pasteur directed experiments and was able to look down his microscope to see the results. The movements of his leg and arm slowly improved.

By the season of 1869 Pasteur was eager to get proof that the silkworm disease was due to a preventable infection. He sent four samples of seed to the Silk Commission of Lyons. One was healthy, and Pasteur predicted that it would hatch normally. The second was infected and Pasteur predicted that all the insects would die of *pébrine*. The third was infected with another disease called *flachery*. Pasteur predicted that this too would perish. The fourth was a mixture of seeds infected with *pébrine* and *flachery*.

The results were just as Pasteur predicted, and the Lyons Commission generously acknowledged that the scourge which had affected their industry for so long was really about to be conquered at last.

6. *The Franco-Prussian War. Fermentation Explained*

The aged Marshal Vaillant was close to the Emperor and was an old frield of Pasteur. He arranged that Pasteur should go for a long stay to one of the Royal estates, the Villa Vicentina near Trieste, and conduct an experiment on silkworm disease there, which should be decisive. The beautiful and peaceful villa would be ideal for Pasteur's convalescence.

The long journey had to be taken in short stages as Pasteur was still a sick man. On arrival Pasteur set to work on his experiment. It was successful.

The government wished to do for Pasteur what it had already done for his famous predecessors Dumas and Claude Bernard, namely to give him a seat in the Senate. The complicated arrangements for this were started. Meanwhile Pasteur and his family spent the winter of 1869–70 at the Villa Vicentina, where his strength improved from day to day.

German students leaving for the Franco-Prussian War (*above*)

The Villa Vicentina near Trieste in Italy where Pasteur convalesced and continued his work on silkworm disease (*left*)

On his way home Pasteur spent two days in Strasbourg. The city was full of rumours of the coming war with Germany. Those who knew the situation well were aware that the Prussians had been building up their army for some time, but that France had sadly neglected her defence.

Pasteur was alarmed at the threat to his country and to his work. On his return to Paris he found that his son had enlisted as had every one of the students of the Ecole Normale. Pasteur wished to join the National Guard, and had to be reminded that his paralysis rendered him unfit for active service.

When the war started Pasteur continued his work. His friends strongly advised him to leave Paris, which was threatened with a siege. On September 5th 1870 he reluctantly started for Arbois. He tried to get solace from his beloved books. However, the misfortunes that were daily befalling France were too much of a distraction. He found it very hard to settle down to any useful work while Paris was being encircled by an overwhelming force of Prussian soldiers.

The Franco-Prussian War brought tragedy and

The bombardment of Villiers during the Franco-Prussian War (*right*)

cruelty on a vast scale to France. There was not enough food for the starving population of Paris, and thousands of children died of starvation and infection. In surgery a new era, the era of antiseptics, had started. However, the brilliant work of Lister and his followers had not yet reached the French Army surgeons, who were in any case overwhelmed by the huge numbers of casualties. Nearly all the soldiers and civilians wounded during the siege of Paris became infected and died of suppuration.

The Prussians showed no mercy for humanity or for culture. On January 8th, 1871, the Prussian Army bombarded the Museum of Natural History in Paris. On learning about the bombardment, Pasteur sent his diploma of Doctor of Medicine back to the University of Bonn. He wrote, "The sight of the parchment is hateful to me and I feel offended at seeing my name, with the qualification of *Virum Clarissimum* that you have given it, placed under a name which is from now on an object of loathing to my country, that of Kaiser Wilhelm." He continued: "My conscience calls on me to ask you to remove my name from the archives of your Faculty and to take back the diploma, as a symbol of the indignation inspired in a French scientist by the barbarity and hypocrisy of the man who persists in the massacre of two great nations in order to satisfy his criminal pride."

Pasteur's son was in the defeated Eastern Army Corps, which was now returning in disorder from the front. Was he alive or dead? And where was he to be found? Pasteur went to look for him among the straggling retreating soldiers. By great good fortune he came upon him, ill, in a rough cart on the road.

Pasteur went to Geneva with his son, who recovered from his illness and went back to France to rejoin his regiment in the early days of February 1871. By now an armistice had been signed with the

The French surrender to the Prussian forces at Sedan in 1870

Cleansing Paris after the departure of the occupation troops in March 1871

Germans and Pasteur wanted to return to Paris. Before he could get there, civil war broke out, and the Commune took over the government of the city.

Pasteur returned to his research on the fermentation of beer. In September 1871 he visited London for the first time to study beer production in England. He was very courteously received and soon convinced the British that the diseases of beer which were causing so much spoilage were due to infection of the yeasts.

On leaving London, Pasteur returned to Paris where his old friend Bertin welcomed him with delight. Paris was slowly recovering from the wounds of war and civil war, and at last Pasteur was able to settle down again to his laboratory work.

After more studies, Pasteur laid down three important principles about beer spoilage:

1. Every alteration of either the wort or the beer itself is due to the development of microbes which are the cause of the disease.
2. These microbes are brought in by the air, by the ingredients of the beer, or by the apparatus used in breweries.
3. Beer which contains no living germs is not subject to disease and will not deteriorate.

These principles were accepted all over the world. Just as heating could preserve wine from deterioration due to various causes, so could bottled beer be preserved by being brought to a temperature of 50–55°. This process became known as Pasteurization and of course it is widely used to this day—most people are familiar with pasteurized milk, which has undergone a similar treatment in order to destroy

French hospital ward in 1892

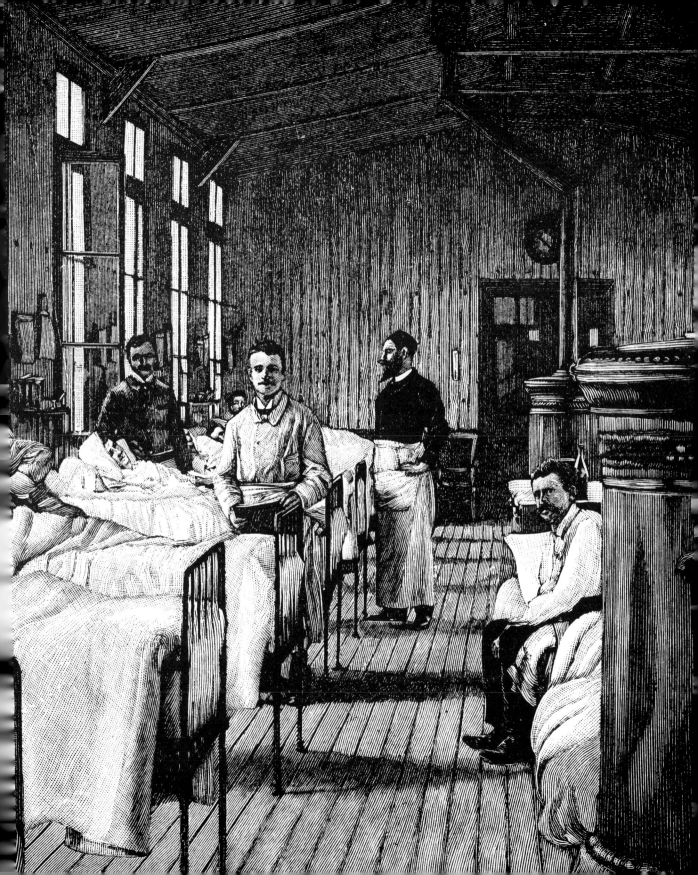

any microbes it may contain.

Pasteur foresaw that his work on infections of beer would have important applications to human disease. In his book on beer, he wrote: "When we see beer and wine undergoing profound changes because they have given refuge to microbes which have been introduced invisibly, and which are now swarming within them, it is impossible not to be haunted by the thought that similar processes may, indeed must, take place in animals and man." In this way the germ theory of infectious diseases was born.

At about this time, the German chemist Liebig disputed Pasteur's statement that the change from wine to vinegar was due to the action of a yeast called *Mycoderma aceti*. This led to a long controversy. So also did Pasteur's contention that the conversion of grape juice to alcohol, that is to say the production of wine, was due to *Mycoderma vini*. This was the name of the yeast which fermented the alcohol.

Pasteur found that some yeasts were aerobic, that is to say, creatures for whose life and development air or rather oxygen was necessary. Others were anaerobic and lived without oxygen. While some microbes were either aerobic or anaerobic and could not be converted to the other form of existence, there were others which could live either way. Into this group came the yeasts of fermentation. They are called "facultative anaerobes." "Fermentation," said Pasteur, "is life without air."

This new theory raised yet another chorus of controversy. Eventually, however, Pasteur's views were accepted and it became possible to lay down some new facts about the causes of fermentation such as the following: (1) that ferments are living microbes (2) that each kind of fermentation is caused by a different microbe, and (3) that these microbes do not arise spontaneously, but develop from other microbes which are already in existence.

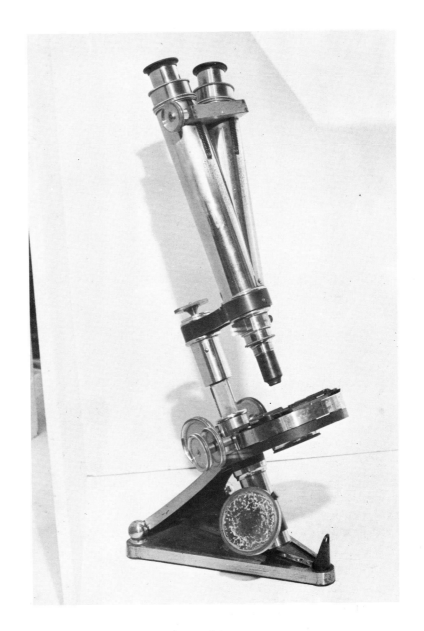

Microscope presented to Pasteur in
1873 by Whitbread's when he was
called to England to investigate
some brewing difficulties

7. *Infectious Diseases*

After his work on yeasts Pasteur decided to study the causes of infectious disease. Many factors drove him to this—his natural humanity, the memory of the children he had lost, and compassionate thoughts of the thousands of young men lost to France every year, especially during the recent war, who were victims of the microscopic germs of killing diseases.

He deeply regretted that he was not a medical man. If he had been, his task would have been much easier, since of course he had to work with medical doctors and persuade them of the truth of his ideas. Fortunately, at the beginning of 1873, an unexpected vacancy occurred in the Academy of Medicine. Pasteur was elected, and this helped to make up for his lack of a medical degree.

As soon as Pasteur was elected he determined to be a most conscientious and punctual academician. His pleasure in election was much increased by the fact that he would be joining his great friend and colleague Claude Bernard. For a long time the latter had been saddened by the hostility of doctors working in hospitals to those who worked in laboratories.

Claude Bernard was convinced that the application of experimental science would enable medicine to emerge from quackery. "We shall not live to see the blossoming out of scientific medicine," he said, "But such is the fate of humanity. Those who sow seeds on the fields of science are not destined to reap

Dr. Robert Koch in his laboratory in 1891. In 1882 Koch discovered the bacillus which causes tuberculosis

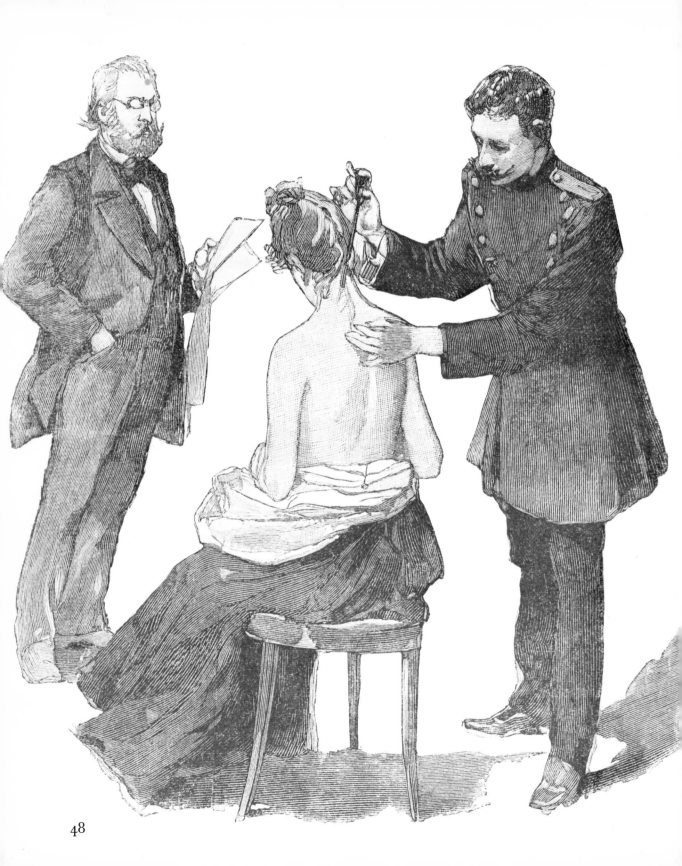

the fruits of their labours."

It is indeed difficult for us to get inside the minds of medical people at the time. In the years 1865 to 1869 Villemin proved that tuberculosis was a disease which reproduced itself, and could not be reproduced except by itself. In other words it was specific and contagious, and could be inoculated from one person to another. He was treated by most of the rather conservative medical profession as if he were a wild revolutionary. In fact, he was a quiet, modest and gentle man.

Villemin had not discovered the bacillus of tuberculosis. This was not achieved until later by Dr. Robert Koch in 1882. But Villemin suspected that such a germ existed. He experimented on animals, inoculating them with tuberculous material. He took the sputum of tuberculous patients, spread it on cotton wool, dried it, and then made the cotton wool into a bed for young guinea-pigs, which contracted the disease soon afterwards.

His opponent, Dr. Pidoux, ridiculed Villemin's ideas, which resembled Pasteur's picture of germs floating about in the air. "Is it not better," said Pidoux, "to follow the truer and more philosophical doctrine of spontaneous decay? Tuberculosis is due to the spontaneous decay of the body under the influence of numerous causes, which we have to look for everywhere to cut down the evil to its roots."

He commented ironically on Villemin's theory that tuberculosis was due to a microbe: "Then all we doctors have to do is to set our nets to catch the germs of tuberculosis and find a vaccine!" As it turned out, this sarcastic remark was quite correct.

Inoculation for tuberculosis. This was known as the Koch treatment

49

8. *Antisepsis and the Healing of Wounds*

People in different branches of medicine and veterinary work now began to think about Pasteur's theories of infectious disease, and to apply them to their own work.

Dr. Davaine was studying anthrax, a very serious disease of farm animals which developed infection of the blood stream, or septicaemia. Davaine had observed that the blood of the sick animals contained small parasites which were visible under a microscope. These were the anthrax bacilli. After studying Pasteur's writings Davaine concluded that these bacteria were the cause of the disease.

Davaine was violently attacked for his views. The controversy grew and many leading doctors took part. The traditional hospital doctors ridiculed the ideas of scientists, who, they said, should know and keep to their place in the scheme of things. This was a humble place.

"Laboratory surgery has destroyed very many animals and saved very few human beings. Laboratory results should be brought out in a careful, modest and reserved manner." So spoke a well-known surgeon, Dr. Chassaignac, to the Academy of Medicine.

The old guard still maintained that putrid infection was not due to living germs. They believed that the putrid odours—the "miasma"—themselves caused the disease. People had already forgotten the words of the great Trousseau, who had died five years before, in 1867: "Every ferment is a germ . . . the variolous ferment produces variolic fermentation (smallpox) giving birth to thousands of pustules, and likewise the microbe of glanders, that of sheep pox, *etc.* . . Other microbes appear to act locally, but

nevertheless they ultimately alter the whole organism, as do gangrene, malignant pustules, contagious erysipelas, and so on. These microbes can be carried about by the lancet, by the atmosphere, or by linen bandages."

Looking back at this violent controversy, we can see that Pasteur was one of a band of forward-looking doctors, who were all thinking the same way. As always in science, progress is not made by the efforts of a single individual, but by the change of the climate of opinion brought about by advances made by all the leaders in the field.

Speaking in the Academy, Pasteur recalled his own researches on lactic and butyric fermentations and on beer. Beer was altered by the presence of microbes infecting the yeasts. If beer becomes altered, it is because it contains organised ferments—microbes. "The correlation between the disease and the presence of microbes is certain, and indisputable. So it is with human disease."

Today we have largely overcome septic infection in hospitals. If such cases occur at all they are unusual. There is an elaborate routine, and a complicated organization, to prevent them.

But in Pasteur's time it was quite different. Hospitals were hotbeds of infection. During the war of 1870 it was agonizing for any sensitive person to work in the casualty wards. The wounds of all the patients were suppurating; a horrible stink pervaded the atmosphere and infectious septicaemia was all over the place. "Pus seemed to germinate everywhere, as if it had been sown by the surgeon." So wrote Landouzy, a medical student of the time.

Pasteur in his laboratory in 1885

Denonvilliers, a surgeon, said to his pupils, "When an amputation seems necessary, think ten times before you decide to do it. Too often, when we decide upon an operation we are just signing the patient's death warrant." For the wound would almost certainly become infected; the patient would develop septicaemia, and die. We must remember that this was long before the days of penicillin and other antibiotics which we now take for granted. Doctors then had no effective way of treating serious infections.

During the siege of Paris, the famous surgeon Nélaton worked in the Grand Hôtel, which had been converted into a hospital. He was in despair as he witnessed the death of almost every patient who had been operated on. "He who conquers purulent infection would deserve a golden statue," he declared.

At the end of the war, Alphonse Guérin observed: "Perhaps the cause of purulent infection may be the germs or ferments discovered by Pasteur to exist in the air. If miasmas are ferments, I might protect the wounded from their fatal influence by filtering the air, as Pasteur did. The idea of cotton wool dressings then came to me and I had the satisfaction of seeing my anticipations realized."

Guérin's method was as follows: he arrested the bleeding, ligatured the blood vessels, and carefully washed the wound with carbolic solution or camphorated alcohol. Then he applied layers of cotton wool, binding the wound with linen bandages. He left the dressings for about 20 days.

Out of 34 patients treated in this way in June 1871, 19 survived. Surgeons were amazed at this survival rate. They could hardly believe it. Dr. Reclus wrote, "We had grown to look on purulent infection as an inevitable and necessary disease, an almost divinely instituted consequence of any important operation."

Even more dangerous than atmospheric germs

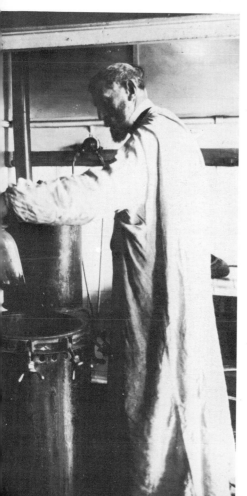

were what were called "contagium germs," such as the surgeon's hands, sponges, and instruments. Infinite precautions have to be taken against them today; they were not even thought of then. Filthy used dressings were left lying about in contact with vessels used in surgical operations. During the Franco-Prussian War, surgeons began to wash wounds carefully and reduced the frequency of dressings. Even these simple measures produced better results.

In 1873 Guérin invited Pasteur to see his methods. Pasteur gladly accepted. This was the beginning of a new period in which he made many visits to hospitals, and had practical discussions with his medical colleagues.

Pasteur was delighted at the thought that he had been a means of awakening in other people ideas likely to lead to the good of humanity. This joy was increased by a letter he received from Lister early in 1874.

Joseph Lister was Professor of Surgery in Edinburgh. He was a thoughtful man, who read a great deal of medical and scientific literature. For years he had been trying to find a way to reduce the numbers of his patients who developed sepsis after operations, all too often with fatal results. He had come to the conclusion that sepsis was due to the putrefaction of wounds by microbes. This was the letter he wrote to Pasteur—it has now become famous.

"My dear Sir,

"Allow me to offer you a pamphlet . . . which contains an account of some investigations into

Pasteur's laboratory (*top*)

Pasteur at work with an early version of his sterilizer (*below*)

54

Joseph Lister as a young man (*left*)
of 28

the subject which you have done so much to elucidate, the theory of germs and of fermentation . . .

"I do not know whether the records of British surgery ever meet your eye. If so, you will have seen from time to time notices of the antiseptic system of treatment which I have been trying for the past nine years to bring to perfection.

"Allow me to take this opportunity to tender you my most cordial thanks for having, by your brilliant researches, demonstrated to me the truth of the germ theory of putrefaction, and thus furnishing me with the principles upon which alone the antiseptic system can be carried out . . ."

In Lister's wards the instruments, sponges, and all the other articles used in dressings were dipped before use in a strong solution of carbolic acid. The surgeon and his assistants scrubbed and carbolized their hands. During every operation, a carbolic acid spray played on to the wound. After the operation the wound was again washed with carbolic solution. Antiseptic materials were used for dressings.

A French medical student, Lucas-Championnière, described Lister's methods in French medical journ-

The school entrance and Pasteur's laboratory

als and later became an exponent of them. The first principles of defence against gangrene, he said, were "extreme and minute care in the dressing of wounds." However, nobody took much notice of him, or of a lecture given by Lister in France at the beginning of 1870. The heads of the profession there, as elsewhere, had absolute confidence in themselves and few people at that time showed any interest in the rumours of success obtained by the antiseptic method. Yet between 1867 and 1869, 34 of Lister's patients out of 40 had survived amputation—success which was quite unprecedented.

Even in his own country Lister was violently attacked. He let the stupid critics talk away and replied by painstakingly improving his methods. With calm courage and smiling kindliness, he tested each step carefully, going over every detail. Like Pasteur, Lister was a man of the greatest fortitude, determination and courage. Pasteur was delighted to find such an ally. He enthusiastically adopted Lister's teachings and did his best to pass them on to others.

Pasteur's experiments have a very modern air: "To demonstrate the bad effects of ferments and microbes on the suppuration of wounds, I would make two identical wounds on two symmetrical limbs of an animal under chloroform. To one of these I would apply a cotton wool dressing with every possible precaution. On the other I would place microbes taken from a septic wound.

"I should like to cut open a wound on an animal under chloroform in a very carefully selected part of the body and in absolutely pure air, that is, air quite free from any kind of germ, after which I would maintain a pure atmosphere around the wound. I am inclined to think that perfect healing would follow under such conditions, for there would be nothing to hinder the work of repair and organisation

which must be completed on the surface of a wound if it is to heal." This is, of course, an account of aseptic, as distinct from antiseptic, surgery.

Pasteur patiently showed the advantages of taking infinite precautions for cleanliness and destroying infectious germs. His struggles in the Academy of Medicine were long and painful, but eventually he succeeded in convincing his colleagues.

In 1874 Dr. Roger, the Annual Secretary of the Academy of Medicine, applied to the government for a special grant for Pasteur to enable him to continue his researches into "the infinitely small." The bill was passed by a huge majority. This was only the third time in the nineteenth century that the government had made such a special grant.

Thereafter Pasteur's annuity relieved him from all financial worry, and recompensed him for having to give up his Professorship at the Sorbonne owing to ill health. He was working at the Ecole Normale, leading a regular life with an even tenor.

In 1876 he went to an International Congress of Silk Culture in Milan and took the opportunity to visit many institutes where his methods of protecting silkworms from disease had been adopted. It was a triumphant and happy voyage, in which he was welcomed everywhere as a great benefactor. At last his efforts were meeting their just reward.

Louis Pasteur at the age of sixty-two

9. *Anthrax and Fowl Cholera and their Prevention*

Pasteur now took up the study of charbon or splenic fever, which today we call anthrax. This disease was ruining agriculture. Many French provinces lost thousands of cattle every year. In the Beauce, for instance, one sheep out of five died in one particular flock. In some parts of the Auvergne, the proportion of deaths was always at least 10 or 15 per cent and sometimes it rose to 50 per cent.

Animals stricken with the disease died of an acute illness within a few hours. Their blood was thickened and darker in colour than normal. The spleen enlarged to an enormous size, hence the name "splenic fever." Men, too, easily caught this dang-

This photograph shows an anthrax infection on the neck of a groundsman who had become infected after spreading fertilizer made from the bones of infected animals. The two pictures on the left show the infection after three days swelling, and on the right after three weeks treatment (*right*)

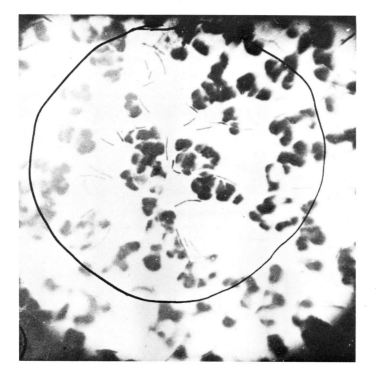

Anthrax bacilli, very greatly magnified. The anthrax bacilli show up as short dark lines. This photograph, supplied by the Pasteur Institute, was taken on 20th March, 1885 (*left*)

58

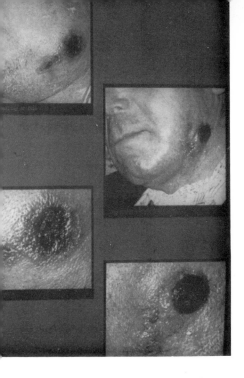

Dr. Robert Koch, German physician (*right*)

erous infection from animals. A pinprick or scratch was often enough to inoculate shepherds, butchers, knackers or farmers. Even people who did not work on farms might get the infection from contaminated shaving brushes and the like. Meat porters picked up the infection from sides of meat. Women might get it from infected furs. Once contracted, the disease developed into septicaemia and most of the patients succumbed.

As long ago as 1838 the veterinary Professor Delafond had pointed out that the blood of affected animals contained little rods, as he called them. These were, of course, the bacilli of anthrax. However, most people regarded this discovery as of no importance.

A young German physician, Robert Koch, became interested in this disease in 1870. He showed that the bacilli, which were now called *Bacillus anthracis*, would produce the disease when inoculated into guinea-pigs, rabbits and mice.

Pasteur now tackled the problem. He took a small drop of blood from an animal which had died of anthrax and put it into a liquid culture medium. The resulting growth of bacteria produced anthrax in rabbits.

After several more experiments Pasteur was able to declare: "Anthrax is caused by the bacillus, just as trichinosis is caused by the trichina and itch by its special acarus—with this difference, that in anthrax the parasite can only be seen through a microscope and very much enlarged."

Pasteur's studies of animals with anthrax went on for many years. He was trying to find a way of preventing the disease, and he succeeded, as we shall see later. It was dangerous work—any infection in the laboratory was likely to prove fatal. Even a slight cut on the hand by a scalpel, while an animal was being dissected, could kill a laboratory worker. But Pasteur and his colleagues carried on, in spite of the personal danger to themselves—an aspect of their work which is often forgotten today now that we have powerful antibiotics, which can prevent so many diseases from developing or cure them when they are established.

During this work Pasteur coined the word "microbe" to denote the microscopic creatures which he had shown to be the cause of so many diseases. The rest of the world followed his example.

Pasteur was now dividing his time equally between the hospital and the laboratory. He tackled every problem of infection as it arose. Childbed fever became another of his interests. He was now working more fruitfully and effectively than ever. His children were grown up, his sons and daughter were married, and he had several grandchildren. He had recovered well from his paralysis. He gave many lectures in institutes in various countries and published many papers and books on his researches.

Pasteur was no cold-blooded aloof intellectual. His friend Roux once wrote: "It is a characteristic of exalted minds to put passion into ideas"—this was an excellent description of Pasteur. He had to fight ignorance, prejudice, the innate conservatism of his eminent colleagues and of the medical establishment. He fought this fight, with kindness, good humour, and a basic equanimity, which yet allowed the passion of his "exalted mind" to drive him on and to inspire other and lesser men with some of his own enthusiasm.

Pasteur now embarked on a new study of a farmyard infection, fowl cholera. Good sitting hens are suddenly found dead in their coops. They stagger around drowsily until they fall dead in agony.

Dr. Emile Roux, French bacteriologist (*right*)

In 1869 a veterinary surgeon named Mortiz had observed some microbes in the blood of stricken animals. His work was studied by Toussaint, who showed that these were the cause of the disease.

Toussaint sent Pasteur the head of a cock that had died of cholera and Pasteur grew the microbes from it. He showed that they produced only a mild disease in guinea-pigs, which he used for further studies in the laboratories. Soon Pasteur was able to devise a culture medium which was suitable for growing the organisms in the laboratory.

Pasteur now made a big discovery. If chicks were inoculated with a laboratory culture which was only one or two days old, they would develop the disease and die. One day, however, Pasteur inoculated some with a culture that had been put away in a cupboard in the laboratory a few weeks before and forgotten. The chicks became ill, but recovered. After they had got better, Pasteur injected one of his virulent cultures into them. The chicks remained resistant and did not die of the disease.

While the neglected culture had been stored in the laboratory, something had happened to weaken it, so that it could no longer cause a fatal disease in chicks. Chicks inoculated with this, however, became resistant to the virulent cultures. This weakening of the microbe, or "attenuation," was clearly an observation of the greatest importance because it opened the way to the possibility of preparing vaccines against a number of microbes by growing them artificially in the laboratory and so weakening them.

This is a supreme example of the importance of a chance observation to the mind of a great man, who was ready to see its significance. "Chance favours only the prepared mind"—an occurrence which ordinary people might have dismissed as of no importance is seen to be significant by a man of genius, and to open up the greatest possi-

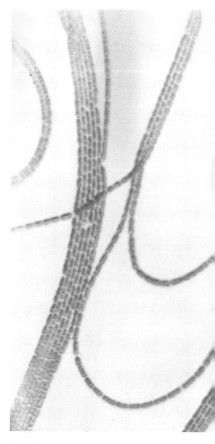

Anthrax bacilli magnified 1500 times

bilities. One thinks at once of the observation by Alexander Fleming, some fifty years later, that in an old and mouldy culture of staphylococci the mould appeared to be killing the bacteria. This led directly to the discovery of penicillin.

Pasteur saw that his observations on chicken cholera led to the possibility of preparing vaccines against other animal diseases, such as anthrax, and so conquering them. More important, the dazzling prospect opened up of protecting humanity from the epidemic diseases which were then threatening whole populations in all countries.

Pasteur plunged with enthusiasm into the work of developing his vaccines, and, equally important, of convincing other scientists that his methods were worth intensive study because of their possible importance. He discovered a microbe in the blood of sufferers from the plague and set about the difficult task of finding a culture medium suitable for growing this in the laboratory.

Meanwhile, Pasteur was still studying the cause of splenic fever, or anthrax, in farm animals. One day he was on a visit to a farm near Chartres where he often went to observe the sick animals. He noticed that the soil in one place had a different colour from that in the rest of the farm. He asked the owner of the farm if he could explain this, and the owner replied that a sheep dead of anthrax had been buried there the year before. Pasteur examined this ground carefully, and found that it contained many of the little cylinders of earth which earthworms deposit in the soil.

The idea at once came to Pasteur that perhaps the earthworms carried the anthrax microbes from the infected field to other areas, and so spread the disease to other animals. As usual, he wasted no time on further speculation, but decided to test this idea in his laboratory. He took back to Paris a number of earthworms from the infected soil,

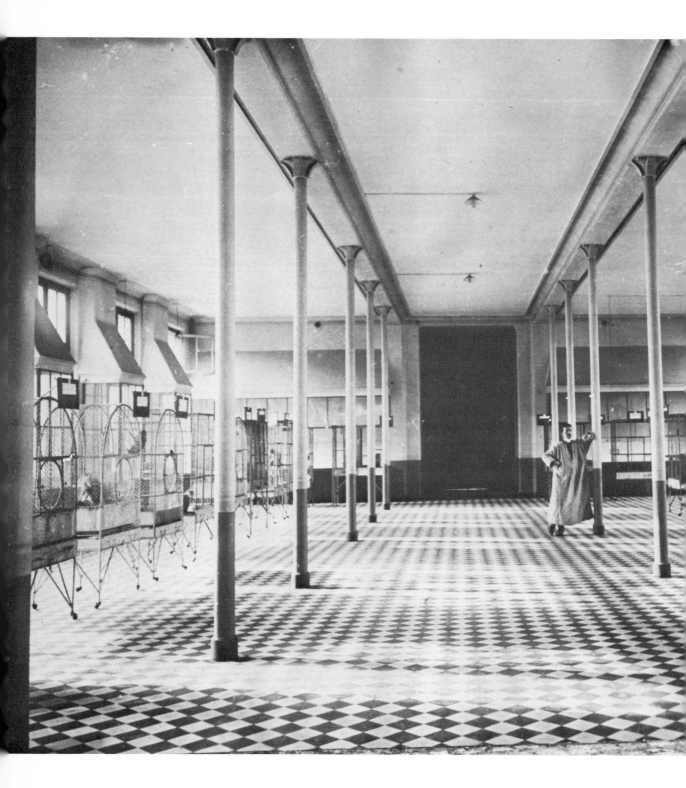

dissected them, and found the spores of the anthrax bacillus in the cylinders of earth in their intestines. Thus did he reveal that earthworms were responsible for the spread of anthrax.

Clearly, it was dangerous to bury animals dead of anthrax in land where the earthworms might pick up the infection from them and convey it elsewhere. So Pasteur recommended that the corpses of animals be buried not in rich pasture meadows but in sandy or chalky soil, which was poor and dry and unsuitable for the growth of earthworms.

There remained the problem of protecting animals and Pasteur continued his efforts to produce a vaccine by attenuating or weakening the organisms artificially. At last, in February 1881, Pasteur thought he had succeeded. Now the vaccine had to be tried out.

The farmers of the agricultural society of Melun, near Paris, organized a trial, and put sixty sheep at Pasteur's disposal.

Pasteur devised his experiment thus: twenty-five of the sheep were to be given two injections of his attenuated vaccine at an interval of fifteen days. These were then to be inoculated with a very virulent anthrax culture. Twenty-five unvaccinated sheep were to be inoculated at the same time with the same culture. These animals would afterwards be compared with the remaining ten sheep who had undergone no treatment at all.

"The twenty-five unvaccinated sheep will all die," Pasteur predicted, "and the vaccinated sheep will survive." Later, ten cows were added to the trial; six were to be vaccinated and four left un-vaccinated.

This crucial experiment was conducted in a full

Pasteur in an animal room.
Animals commonly used for
experiments were rabbits, mice,
monkeys and guinea-pigs

65

blaze of publicity, which left no room for a doubtful result. If it succeeded, Pasteur would be triumphantly justified in the eyes of the world; it if failed, he would be discredited and ridiculed. But Pasteur did not flinch. His careful and painstaking work had convinced him and given him the courage of his convictions. Such supreme self-confidence and the ability to put himself well and truly on the spot in this way was characteristic of him, as it is of all really great men.

The experiment eventually took place in May 1881. On May 5th the test animals were given their first injection; the second followed twelve days later. On May 31st all the animals were inoculated with the virulent culture. Vaccinated and unvaccinated animals were separated in different fields and the anxious wait began.

On June 2nd Pasteur received a telegram from Melun—all the unvaccinated animals had died of anthrax, and all the vaccinated animals were alive and well.

Pasteur rushed to Melun, where a large crowd had gathered. As he arrived at the farmyard with his young collaborators a roar of applause broke out. His triumph was complete. Anthrax was conquered at last. Veterinary surgeons and farmers hurried to protect animals with the new method.

Honours were showered on Pasteur. The government bestowed on him the Grand Ribbon of the Legion of Honour. Then came a further triumph. In August Pasteur was invited to represent his country at the International Medical Congress in London. As he arrived at St. James' Hall, filled to overflowing with delegates from all over the world, cheers broke out. Pasteur was the great success of the Congress. The English took to him immediately, good as they are in recognizing courage in great men. Back in France, Pasteur was elected one of the "immortals" of the French Academy.

Pasteur wearing the Grand Ribbon of the Legion of Honour

10. *The Triumph over Rabies*

The whole world began to enjoy the benefits of Pasteur's discoveries. In the year 1882, in France alone, more than half a million sheep and 80,000 oxen were vaccinated against anthrax. Farmers saved millions of francs which they had lost from the disease in previous years. The great English physiologist Thomas Henry Huxley declared in a public lecture at the Royal Society in London: "Pasteur's discoveries alone would suffice to cover the war indemnity of five milliards paid by France to Germany in 1870."

Pasteur as Professor at the Ecole Normale (*below left*)

Establishment set up for the preparation of rabies vaccine (*below*)

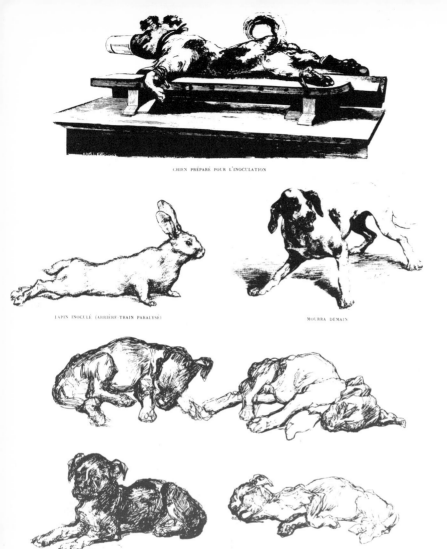

CHIEN PRÉPARÉ POUR L'INOCULATION

LAPIN INOCULÉ (ARRIÈRE-TRAIN PARALYSÉ)

MOURRA DEMAIN

Illustrations from a Paris newspaper in 1884 showing various aspects of Pasteur's experiments on rabies in animals

Meanwhile Pasteur's previous discoveries were saving countless human lives. Since the antiseptic method had been introduced into surgery, the mortality of operations in hospitals had fallen from 50 to 5 per cent. In maternity hospitals, where the mortality had previously been 10 to 20 per cent, it was now less than 3 per thousand.

Yet problems multiplied also. Swine fever was a disease of pigs which caused great damage, and Pasteur embarked on the study of this. Cholera was advancing in Egypt, and threatened the city of

CAGE OU SONT ENFERMÉS LES CHIENS INOCULÉS

L'INOCULATION CAUSE UNE GRANDE AGITATION.

Alexandria. Pasteur went there to study it in 1883. Unexpectedly, the epidemic ceased, and Pasteur went back to France.

Another vast problem presented itself, that of rabies. Many dogs in every country were afflicted with this fatal disease, which was a perpetual danger to human beings who might be bitten by them. People could also develop the disease without being bitten; a lick from a sick dog's tongue was enough. Nor were dogs the only dangerous animals. Wolves, jackals, and other carnivores were also affected and could transmit the disease to human beings in the same way.

The human disease was often called "hydrophobia," from the Greek words meaning "fear of water." It is an inflammation of the brain in which the patients become very excitable. Even the sound of running water, as from an ordinary tap, may be enough to being on an attack of morbid excitement, hence the name.

Rabies in both humans and animals was, and still is, a most serious disease; recovery is almost unheard of. It had been shown in 1870 that the infectious agent was present in the saliva of sick animals. Pasteur studied the saliva of dogs and of human beings who died of the disease, and confirmed the presence of the infectious agent in them. He then made a crucial discovery—that the agent of rabies was also to be found in the dog's brain and spinal cord.

Was it possible to attenuate this in the same way as the anthrax bacillus had been attenuated?

Pasteur set to work. He removed the medulla from the brain of a rabbit which had died of rabies and suspended it in a sterilized phial for fourteen days. Pasteur then made an extract of the dried tissue and injected it into dogs. They did not develop rabies. Next day he injected the dogs with an extract of medulla which had been dried for thirteen

Pasteur experimenting on a chloroformed rabbit. Chloroform was used to put animals to sleep to stop them struggling

days, and the following day with a twelve day extract, and so on. Then he allowed these dogs to be bitten by rabid animals. The inoculated animals did not develop rabies. Pasteur's process of drying the medulla had successfully attenuated the microbe. These extracts could perhaps now be used to protect human beings and animals.

Pasteur was anxious that his findings be verified, and a special commission was set up for this purpose. Experiments were conducted on hundreds of animals, which confirmed Pasteur's findings. Could human beings be protected in the same way?

On Monday, July 6th, 1885, a little Alsatian boy named Joseph Meister entered Pasteur's laboratory with his mother. Two days before he had been bitten by a mad dog, and the mother was distraught. Human beings never recovered once they had developed rabies; the disease was always fatal. Could anything be done to save the child?

Pasteur was not yet ready to try his vaccine on human beings. What should he do? Should he do nothing and let the boy die? Should he risk his

Joseph Meister being bitten by the mad dog (*left*)

Pasteur with a group of English children who had been bitten by dogs and sent to him for inoculation (*top right*)

The opening of the new Pasteur Institute in Paris by President Carnot in 1888 (*below right*)

THE VIVISECTION LABORATORY

EXTERIOR OF THE INST

External view of the Pasteur Institute

vaccine on Joseph, who might die in any case, when Pasteur would be discredited and, very probably, blamed for the child's death? Yet he felt in his bones that his vaccine could save Joseph.

Pasteur consulted two senior and discreet medical colleagues. They advised him to go ahead and vaccinate the boy. He did. In ten days Joseph received twelve injections of vaccine, ending up with an extract of medulla which was only one day old and therefore almost fully virulent.

Joseph remained well and went home a few days later. Rabies was conquered. And once again, Pasteur had had the courage to put his theories to the most crucial test and had triumphed.

The news flashed around the world. From all over Europe, farmers and peasants who had been bitten by rabid dogs and wolves began to stream into Paris to receive Pasteur's treatment.

The Academy of Sciences recommended that an institute, to be known as the Pasteur Institute, be set up to organize the preventive treatment of rabies. They opened a subscription list in France and other countries. Immediately money started pouring in from all over the world. This was the beginning of what has become the most famous institute anywhere for the study of microbes and the prevention of microbial disease.

The Institute soon extended its field of activity to other subjects in microbiology, and made an enviable name for itself for the excellence of its research. To have done a spell at the Pasteur Institute became a hallmark of excellence for all young microbiologists. Daughter institutes have also been set up in other countries. Our own Lister Institute, bearing the name of Pasteur's famous English colleague and collaborator, is a similar foundation.

By now, Pasteur's name was familiar all over the world. He was asked to attend and to speak at many a charitable and scientific gathering in many different countries. He always agreed to do this whenever he could, for he knew that his presence was a guarantee of success. Like other great men, he was liberal with his help and sympathy for others, especially younger doctors and scientists. He answered countless letters from private people who wrote to him about their problems.

Pasteur moved into the new and splendid laboratories of the Pasteur Institute where he continued his researches. He addressed meetings, wrote scientific papers, attended congresses. As the year 1892 approached, committees in various countries were set up to organise the celebrations for his seventieth birthday. The official reception was held on the morning of the actual day—December 27th.

The Great Hall of the Sorbonne was crowded by notables from all over the world, including delegates from all the leading scientific societies. Pasteur entered leaning on the arm of the President of the Republic. The highlight of this occasion, never to be forgotten by those who saw it, was the moment when Pasteur and Lister embraced one another— two of the greatest men the world has ever known, to each of whom countless lesser mortals owed their lives, and a living symbol of the international brotherhood of science and of collaboration between the wise men of different nations.

Lister greets Pasteur at the Sorbonne

11. *Diphtheria*

Pasteur was now an old man, but he went on working with the vigour of his youth. Yet another problem presented itself, that of diphtheria, which every year killed thousands of children in France and other countries. During outbreaks, entire classes of children might become ill. More than half of those affected died of the disease.

The bacterium which causes the disease was discovered by a German named Klebs in 1883. In the Pasteur Institute it was studied by Dr. Roux and Dr. Yersin, two of Pasteur's assistants. They found that cultures of the microbe contained a toxic

Working Conference on rabies at
Coonor, India. Portions of brain
tissues from animals infected with
rabies are here being weighed prior
to testing (*below*)

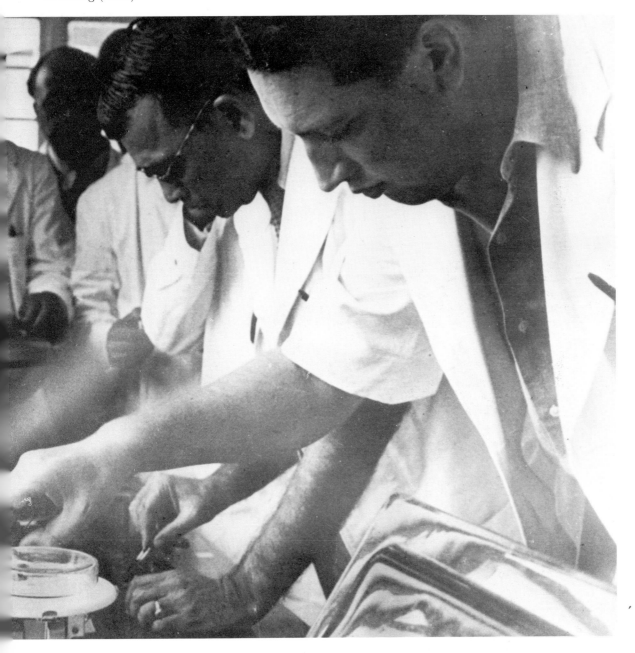

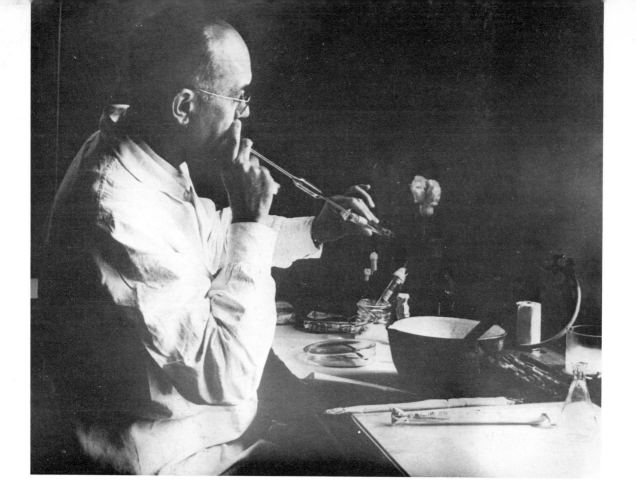

substance, which, when injected into guinea-pigs and other animals, produced in them the signs of diphtheria. This diphtheria toxin was the main weapon whereby the microbe produced disease in human beings.

Dr. Roux found that by adding iodine to the toxin he could reduce its potency. He injected some of this weakened toxin into horses, and found that the horses became immune. Their blood produced an antitoxin which neutralised the virulent toxin.

Roux gave injections of this horse serum to other animals which had previously been infected with

The Coonor Conference. Dr. Pierre Lépine of the Pasteur Institute prepares material for a laboratory training programme (*above*)

Rabies is still a problem in many countries today. Here a young Philippino girl is having her fifteenth injection after being licked on an open wound by an infected dog (*right*)

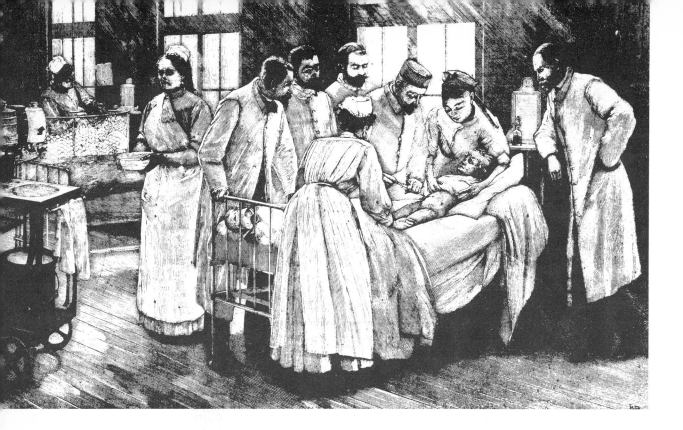

diphtheria bacilli. Then he injected these animals with virulent diphtheria bacilli. The animals did not develop diphtheria, or, if they had already contracted the disease, they recovered.

The next and crucial step was to see if human beings could be cured in the same way. A trial was organized at the one of the two hospitals where diphtheritic children were admitted. In the other hospital, the old methods of treatment were to continue.

Within four months, after hundreds of children had been given antitoxin, the results were evident. In the treated children the mortality of diphtheria had been brought down from 51 to 24 per cent. In the others the mortality was 60 per cent.

This was the start of the long fight against diphtheria which has gone on to our own day, and which has resulted, within the past twenty years, in the

Vaccination for diphtheria by the Roux method

Pasteur with two grandchildren at the seaside in 1891 (*right*)

virtual disappearance of this disease from many countries including our own.

In November 1894 Pasteur became ill with kidney failure. After several weeks he slowly started to recover, and his mind, if not his body, regained its normal vigour. As soon as the weather allowed, a tent was set up for him in the garden of the Pasteur Institute, where he went to sit. However, in the spring of 1895 his strength began to diminish visibly. Soon he could hardly walk. He grew weaker and weaker and, on Friday September 27th, 1895, he took to his bed for the last time. Next day he died peacefully, surrounded by his family, colleagues and students.

12. *The Genius of Pasteur*

Circumstances produce the man—sometimes. Sometimes however they do not.

It is true that by the mid-nineteenth century the accepted knowledge about microbes, and the state of medical science, were advanced enough for it to be possible for someone to pull all these threads together as did Pasteur. After all, he was not the first to propound the germ theory of disease, or to advocate antiseptic surgery. Yet how much more difficult would Lister's task have been had Pasteur never lived!

When we think of Pasteur's work on specific problems such as fermentation and the diseases of beer and wine, anthrax, fowl cholera, plague, and rabies—to name but a few—his influence was surely decisive. By now, no doubt, these scourges would have been almost conquered without him. But it would have taken humanity so much longer; countless more lives would have been lost, and all future history would have been different. Again, in Pasteur's time vast problems of human and animal diseases were there to be solved. Pasteur was able to apply the results of his researches immediately and directly. This was all that he was interested in—solving practical problems to help humanity. He was not interested in research which could not be applied to help his fellow men. He would have scorned the idea of "science for science's sake," which is sometimes put forward by people who really have no idea what science is all about.

History is endlessly fascinating. For centuries, historians and philosophers have argued about how important is the individual person in shaping events, and how much he is dependent on his circumstances and his time. If Pasteur had lived in the fifteenth century, what would he have achieved? In the words

Pasteur's deathbed

of Thomas Gray:

"Full many a flower is born to blush unseen,
And waste its sweetness on the desert air."

—though it is hard to imagine that such a man as Pasteur would not have made his mark whenever or wherever he had lived. The fact is, however, that Pasteur did live, at the right time, and we are all enormously the better for his achievements.

But it was not enough for Pasteur to be a great scientist. In order for him to get his discoveries across to his colleagues, to convince the world, he had to be a great human being. He had to have infinite integrity, courage and perseverance—in a word "guts."

The way in which he overcame a most serious illness, paralysis of half of his body, is a supreme example of his courage. No one could have blamed Pasteur if he had just worked part-time when he recovered from paralysis. But no. At the earliest possible moment, he was working as hard as ever, and he continued to do so for the rest of his life.

With this great strength of character, one might have expected Pasteur to be a hard and rigid and difficult person. On the contrary, everyone who knew him testifies to his excellence as a human being on an intimate, homely, personal level. He was kindly, generous, and considerate to his family and his colleagues. His family life was a model of respectability and worthiness. He was tireless in doing all he could to help ordinary people anywhere. He was passionate and excitable—but only in the best of causes.

No one is perfect. Yet it is as foolish to be blind to human excellence as it is to see it everywhere. In the person of Louis Pasteur we can see a mixture of good qualities such as have rarely been found in the entire history of our race. And he lived just at the time and place when it was possible for his work and his example to bear fruit.

One of the last photographs taken of Pasteur. He is seen here with some of his fellow workers in the library of the Pasteur Institute

The lessons of Pasteur's life, for us, may be trite, but they are none the less true and telling.

So, to end with more of the words of the same poem of Longfellow with which we began:

"Let us, then, be up and doing,
With a heart for any fate;
Still achieving, still pursuing,
Learn to labour and to wait."

Pasteur's tomb in the Pasteur Institute, Paris

Date Chart

1822	Birth of Louis Pasteur at Dôle on December 27th.
1827	His family move to Arbois.
1838	First visit to Paris.
1839–42	Secondary education at the Royal College at Besançon.
1842	Admitted to Ecole Normale Supérieure in Paris, and left in order to obtain a higher ranking.
1842–43	Studies at the Lycée Saint-Louis, at the Sorbonne, and at the Institut Barbet in Paris.
1843	Readmitted to the Ecole Normale.
1844	Begins chemical and crystallographic studies. Discovery of molecular asymmetry.
1846	Appointed assistant at Ecole Normale.
1847	Qualified as Doctor of Science.
1848	Appointed Professor of Chemistry at University of Strasbourg.
1848	Marriage to Marie Laurent on May 29th.
1850	Birth of daughter, Jeanne.
1851	Birth of son, Jean-Baptiste.
1853	Birth of daughter, Cécile. Awarded Legion of Honour for chemical studies.
1854	Appointed Professor of Chemistry and Dean in the Faculty of Sciences at Lille University.
1855	Beginning of studies on fermentation.
1857	Appointed director of scientific studies at Ecole Normale Supérieure in Paris.
1858	Birth of daughter, Marie-Louise.
1859	Death of daughter, Jeanne.

	Beginning of studies on spontaneous generation.
1861	Discovery of anaerobic life.
1862	Elected to Academy of Sciences.
	Studies on acetic acid fermentation.
1863	Studies on wine.
	Appointed Professor of Geology, Physics and Chemistry at Ecole des Beaux Arts.
	Birth of daughter, Camille.
1864	Publication of "Mémoire sur la fermentation acétique."
	Controversy on spontaneous generation.
	Establishment of field laboratory at Arbois to study wine disease.
1865	Studies on pasteurisation.
	Death of father and of youngest daughter Camille.
1865–9	Begins to study silkworm diseases.
1866	Publication of essay on scientific achievements of Claude Bernard.
	Death of Cécile.
1867	Grand Prix of the Universal Exhibition for method of preservation of wines by heating.
	Appointed Professor of Chemistry at the Sorbonne.
1868	Publication of "Studies on Vinegar."
	Attack of left-sided paralysis in October.
1869	Resumes study of silkworm diseases. Convalescence at Villa Vicentina.
1870	Returns to Paris.
	Franco-Prussian War.
1871	Searches and finds his son.
	Returns to work in Paris at Ecole Normale.
1873	Elected Associate member of the Academy of Medicine.
1876	Candidate for election to Senate but defeated.

	Publication of Studies on Beer.
1877	Begins studies of anthrax.
1878	Studies on gangrene, septicemia, childbirth fever.
1879	Studies on chicken cholera. Discovery of immunisation by means of attenuated cultures.
	Marriage of daughter Marie-Louise to René Vallery-Radot.
1879	Marriage of son Jean-Baptiste.
1880	Begins to study rabies.
1881	Field trial of anthrax vaccination.
1882	Election to Academy.
1883	Vaccination against swine erysipelas. Studies on cholera.
1885	Treatment of Joseph Meister against rabies.
1886	International subscription for foundation of Pasteur Institute.
1888	Inauguration of Pasteur Institute.
1892	Celebration of 70th birthday at the Sorbonne.
1895	Death on 28th September.

Glossary

ANTHRAX   A disease of cattle and humans due to a bacillus.

ANTISEPTIC   A substance which will prevent growth of microbes without necessarily killing them.

ANTISEPTIC SURGERY   Surgical procedure in which antiseptics are liberally used to prevent infection.

ANTITOXIN   Serum containing antibodies, antidote to toxin.

ASEPTIC SURGERY   Surgical procedure in which elaborate precautions are taken to prevent the admission of living microbes to the surgical area.

BACILLI   Rod-shaped microbes.

BUTYRIC ACID   An organic acid found in butter and other substances.

CARBOLIC ACID   The name of a strongly disinfectant chemical substance.

CHILDBED FEVER   A bacterial infection contracted by women in childbirth.

CHOLERA   A specific (q.v.) infection of the small intestine due to a bacillus.

CONTAGIOUS   Disease which is caught by direct physical contact.

DIMORPHIC   A substance which exists in two different structural forms.

DIPHTHERIA   A specific (q.v.) infectious disease which used to be common in childhood.

ECOLE NORMALE   Teacher's training school.

FERMENTATION   Chemical change of sugar to alcohol by yeasts and other similar kinds of chemical change by living organisms.

FLACHERY   An infectious disease of silkworms.

GANGRENE   Death of living tissue.

HYDROPHOBIA   Human rabies.

MALIGNANT PUSTULE   Sore in the skin which occurs

in anthrax.

MEDULLA   Part of the base of the brain.

MIASMA   Foul-smelling gas produced by decaying organic matter.

MICROBE   Living organism so small that it cannot be seen with the naked eye.

MICRO-ORGANISM   Same as microbe.

PEBRINE   An infectious disease of silkworms.

PLAGUE   A specific (q.v.) acute infectious disease caused by a bacillus.

POLARIZED LIGHT   Light which has been altered by being passed through a crystal or solution, so that its rays all travel in the same plane.

PUS   A fluid mixture of white blood cells, other body cells, microbes, produced in infected tissues.

RABIES   A specific (q.v.) infectious disease contracted by humans and animals by contact with infected animals.

SEPSIS   Infection of living tissue.

SEPTICAEMIA   Infection of the blood stream.

SPECIFIC   Produced by a single kind of microbe.

SPONTANEOUS GENERATION   The theory that living organisms can originate from non-living matter.

SUPPURATION   The production of pus in infected tissues.

SWINE ERYSIPELAS   A specific (q.v.) bacterial infection of swine.

TARTARIC ACID   An organic acid found in wine and other substances.

TOXIN   Poisonous substance.

VACCINE   Substance used to immunize people.

VARIOLA   Smallpox.

Further Reading

The best book is:

Vallery-Radot, René (Pasteur's son-in-law), *The Life of Pasteur* (Dover publications, New York, 1960)

Other recommended books:

Dubos, René J., *Louis Pasteur, Freelance of Science* (Gollancz, 1961)

Duclaux, Emile, *Pasteur, the History of a Mind* (W. B. Saunders Company, 1920)

Grant, Madeleine P., *Louis Pasteur—Fighting Hero of Science* (Benn, 1960)

Nicolle, Jacques, *Louis Pasteur, A Master of Scientific Enquiry* (Hutchinson, 1961)

Index

Picture Credits

Acknowledgement is made to the following for kind permission to reproduce illustrations:

Centre d'Optique & d'Electronique for the frontispiece and the illustrations on pages 68–69, 70 and 71.

Mary Evans Picture Library for illustrations on pages 14, 15, 19, 29, 38–39, 41, 42–43, 47, 48, 55, 68, 78, 82.

The Luton and Dunstable Hospital for the upper photograph on page 59.

The Pasteur Institute for illustrations on pages 10, 12, 13, 18, 21, 24–25, 27, 30–31, 32, 38, 59, 62–63, 66, 83, 86.

Paul Popper Ltd. for illustrations on pages 28–29, 75, 84–85, and 87.

The Radio Times Hulton Picture Library for illustrations on pages 11, 26, 34, 45, 50–51, 52–53, 56–57, 64–65, 73, 74, 75, 77.

The Ronan Picture Library for the illustration on page 54.

H. Roger Viollet for illustrations on pages 16, 17, 61 and 76.

The Wellcome Foundation for the illustration on pages 62–63.

The World Health Organisation for illustrations on pages 78–79, 80 and 81.

The author and publisher also wish to thank Faber and Faber Ltd. for permission to quote, in the introduction, from the poem "I think continually of those who were truly great" from *Collected Poems* by Stephen Spender.